Eating
Disorders

Trudi Strain Trueit

Franklin Watts
A Division of Scholastic Inc.
New York • Toronto • London • Auckland • Sydney
Mexico City • New Delhi • Hong Kong
Danbury, Connecticut

Dedication

For everyone who courageously shared their hard-ships, hopes, and hearts to make this book possible.

Cover illustration by Peter Cho.
Cover and interior design by Kathleen Santini.
Illustrations by Pat Rasch.

Library of Congress Cataloging-in-Publication Data

Trueit, Trudi Strain.
  Eating Disorders / Trudi Srain Trueit.
      v. cm. — (Life balance)
Contents: Mirror, mirror—Creating body image—The road to eating disorders—Anorexia: a downward spiral—Battling bulimia and binge eating—Reaching out.
Includes bibliographical references and index.
  ISBN 0-531-12218-2 (lib. bdg.)   0-531-16610-4 (pbk.)
  1. Eating disorders in adolescence—Juvenile literature. [1. Eating diorders. 2. Body image] I. Title. II. Series.
  RJ506.E18T78 2003
  616.85'26—dc21
                                        2003000105

Table of Contents

One

Mirror, Mirror

If you've ever ventured into an amusement park fun-house, you probably laughed at the way the mirrors stretched, squeezed, and squashed your reflection. A fun-house mirror creates silly exaggerations of our bodies that we know aren't true. But what happens when you look into a regular mirror at home? Are you seeing what is really there or an image altered by your own mind?

Your body image is a mental picture of yourself that you see when you gaze into a mirror. Your feelings, experiences, and expectations play a role in the reflection you see. Body image also takes into account what you believe other people think about the way you look. This perception is influenced by many factors, including family, friends, religion, culture, and the media.

Different Views

In a survey of more than two hundred kids aged twelve to fifteen, about 85 percent of boys said they were mostly happy with the way they looked, while less than 40 percent of girls felt satisfied with their bodies.

Twelve-year-old Faith, an A student and a goalie on her soccer team, has seen her body develop earlier than most of her friends. Faith is frustrated by her widening hips, which make it difficult for her to fit into her jeans. Her doctor tells her it is normal for girls to experience weight gain during puberty because hormones—natural chemicals in the body—are released to regulate growth. Faith's friends and family think she looks great and tell her so. But Faith believes that if she could only lose weight, she would be happier and more popular. In frustration, she decides not to go to the seventh-grade dance. "What's the point?" she wonders. "Nobody's going to ask someone so huge to dance anyway. I feel so fat and ugly. I'm totally worthless."

Of course, the reality is that Faith is none of these things. But no one can convince her that she is peering into a fun-house mirror of her own creation and seeing an inaccurate view of herself. Is Faith right? Will fitting into her old jeans make her happier? More popular? Probably not. Sometimes, we focus on appearance—something we think or hope we can change—rather than dealing with the emotions we feel. It is easier for Faith to say, "I'm fat" than it is to admit that she is fearful about her changing body and not being accepted by others. Although she is an excellent student, a top athlete, and has many friends, Faith's negative body image is overwhelming the positive aspects of her life. It is affecting her relationships with others and altering her social behavior. It is making her feel bad not only about how she looks but also about who she is.

Matters of the Mind

All of us can pick out a physical feature or two about ourselves we wish we could change: too many freckles, a crooked smile, ears that stick out, a few extra pounds. But when we become preoccupied with these things, we run the risk of forming a negative body image. This disapproving view can lead to depression, isolation, and low self-esteem. Self-esteem is belief in your overall value as a person. It is what gives you the confidence to believe in yourself, to set and accomplish goals, and to live a joy-filled life. A negative body image can affect your self-esteem,

Self-esteem is what gives you the confidence to believe in yourself, to set and accomplish goals, and to live a joy-filled life.

causing you to question your worth. It may prompt you to make poor nutritional and exercise choices to change your body. Not only will these tactics fail to boost your self-esteem, they can also jeopardize your health.

In a small percentage of the population, a negative body image may contribute to the onset of an eating disorder. Anorexia nervosa, bulimia nervosa, and binge eating disorder (BED) are the three main types of eating disorders. Anorexia nervosa is self-starvation leading to significant weight loss. Bulimia nervosa is characterized by

What's Your Body Image?

- Do you spend a lot of time looking at yourself in the mirror and not liking what you see?
- Do you avoid mirrors altogether?
- Do you hate one or more parts of your body?
- Do you make a special effort to hide the parts of yourself you don't like, such as wearing loose clothes to cover hips, arms, or thighs?
- Do you need constant reassurance from friends and family that you look all right?
- Are you continually saying negative things to yourself, like "I'm ugly" or "I'm fat"?
- Do you compare yourself to others and feel you don't measure up?
- Do you stay home instead of going out because you feel ashamed about how you look?

If you answered "yes" to two or more of the above questions, you may have a problem with negative body image. For tips on how to turn negative thoughts around, see Chapter 7, "Changing the View."

a cycle of bingeing and purging. Bingeing means eating a lot of food at one time. In bulimia, a binge is always followed by a purge, or getting rid of what has been eaten. This is done through self-induced vomiting or by the use of laxatives, enemas, and diuretics; it can also be accomplished by fasting or through excessive exercise. Binge eating disorder (BED) is defined as eating significantly more than what a normal person would eat in one sitting or eating continuously over a long stretch of time. While no purging is involved, someone with BED may fast or diet to try to lose weight.

Rather than eating a nutritious meal when hungry, persons with an eating disorder develop an extreme fear of food and of getting fat. They may adopt an unhealthy view toward eating and/or exercise, which, if left untreated, will result in serious physical and mental consequences. It is important to understand that eating disorders are not simply abnormal attitudes about food. They are mental illnesses, born out of unhealthy habits that have gotten out of hand. People with an eating disorder cannot simply change their view to correct the

Eating disorders are not simply abnormal attitudes about food. They are mental illnesses.

problem, because they are no longer in control of the situation. Someone with anorexia, bulimia, or binge eating disorder is in the throes of a dangerous, and potentially life-threatening, disease.

In the United States, about eight million girls and women and about one million boys and men are currently battling an eating disorder—a figure that has more than doubled over the last 20 years. Yet, these illnesses are preventable. The first step in avoiding an eating disorder is to create a positive body image. This means learning to see your body as it really is, instead of being overly critical about such things as your features, size, shape, and weight. It means respecting yourself so you can feel comfortable in your skin. But most important, it means remembering that *who you are* is far more important than the way you look.

TWO

Creating Body Image

I f you're like most kids, you watch between four and six hours of television each day. That amounts to more than two hundred commercials whizzing past your eyes on a daily basis. Chances are the media plays a big role in how you define your body, because about one-third of advertisements focus on body image to sell a product.

Body Beautiful

In a survey where teens were asked to describe the "ideal body," boys most often said that males should be muscular and tall and should have six-pack abs and low body fat. Girls characterized the ideal female as pretty, skinny, tan, and tall, with a defined waist, thin stomach, blue eyes, and low body fat.

In a national survey of 1,200 kids aged ten to seventeen, seven out of ten girls said that they wanted to look like a television character. Nearly one-third said they had actually changed something about their appearance to be more like that character. On film and television, it may seem as if celebrities are born beautiful. But behind the camera, plenty of hard work goes into keeping that illusion alive. Good lighting, flattering camera angles, and other Hollywood tricks can make stars look younger, more attractive, and thinner than they really are. Entertainers also have makeup artists, costumers, hair stylists, gourmet chefs, and personal trainers to keep them in top form. Some even opt for plastic surgery, going under the knife for liposuction, face-lifts, tummy tucks, and breast enhancements.

Magazines, too, employ professionals to aim for perfection during and after photo shoots. Graphic artists often manipulate photos in print ads and articles to create ideal images. For example, they use computers to alter photos, making models appear taller and thinner than they really are. Software programs can digitally erase wrinkles, scars, birthmarks, freckles, and other "imperfections." Even hair and eye color can be changed with the click of a mouse.

A Thin Obsession

Flip through any fashion magazine and you're likely to see

super skinny supermodels. It may seem as if these slim figures represent the normal body type. Actually, the tall, lean models you see weigh less than 98 percent of the general population. The average model stands 5 feet 11 inches (180 centimeters) tall and weighs 117 pounds (53 kilograms). Contrast that with the average American woman, who measures 5 feet 4 inches (163 cm) and weighs 140 pounds (64 kg). While nearly all models wear a size 6 or smaller, 60 percent of American women wear a size 14 or larger.

Thirteen-year-old Danielle, who is recovering from anorexia, used to believe it was important to look like the models she saw on the pages of magazines and catalogs. She felt that if she were thinner her life would be better. "Everybody in the magazines always seems so happy. The message is that if you're skinnier you'll be happier, boys will like you more, you're going to look great, and you'll have all these advantages. It isn't true. It's all an illusion to sell stuff."

Models themselves admit they often find it difficult to maintain the rigid standards of thinness their profession demands. Kim Alexis, Carol Alt, and Brooke Shields are among those who have revealed that it was only through excessive dieting that they were able to remain so slender.

If you aren't aware that what you're viewing in the media may be more fantasy than fact, you may feel you don't measure up. You may try to be something that isn't realistic. Like eye and hair color, your height, frame, and physical shape are not traits you have much control over. Your body type is determined primarily by genetics, the characteristics you inherited from your parents. Trying to change what nature gave you is a mission that is doomed from the start. At best, it will cause frustration and disappointment. At worst, it may lead to unhealthy eating habits and, possibly, an eating disorder.

The Power of Loved Ones

Perhaps the biggest influence on our body image comes from those that are closest to us. Studies show the feedback we get from family and friends in childhood can affect what we think about ourselves for the rest of our lives. "I was in a dressing room trying on clothes for the new school year," remembers Richelle. "I couldn't fit into the size 7 jeans. I gave them to my mom, and I heard her ask the saleslady for a 9. 'Better get an 11, too,' she said, 'too many pizza parties over the summer.' I was so embarrassed I didn't want to come out of the dressing room."

Without realizing it, parents may be passing down the message that was passed down to them—"thin is good." "I can't ever remember a time when my mother wasn't on some kind of diet," says Holly. "She'd be telling me to finish all the food on my plate, but she'd eat only yogurt for dinner. Eventually, I started dieting, too." It is estimated that 80 percent of girls will have attempted to lose weight by the time they reach eighth grade. Considering that, at any one time, at least half of all American women and one-quarter of American men are on a diet, the simple fact may be that children are merely following in their parents' footsteps.

Friends and classmates can also place demands on you to look or act a certain way. This kind of pressure contributed to Danielle's anorexia. "I used to love to shop," she says. "I always thought, 'I have to get this; I don't care [how much money or effort] it takes.' My friends still shop a lot, but it doesn't interest me anymore because I know the clothes aren't going to affect who I am. You buy a shirt and it gets old in a week, and what seemed so great at the time isn't a big deal anymore."

Friends First

When asked which outside factor most influenced their body image, a majority of the teenage girls who were surveyed said "friends." They rated the opinions of their peers ahead of the media, siblings, and even parents.

Of all the input you receive from the world regarding body image, the most important element is you. *You* decide whether to believe what you read, hear, see, and experience. Your beliefs about your appearance can lead you down either a positive road or a negative one. Which path will you choose?

What Do You See?

Look at the self-portraits on these pages drawn by eighth and ninth graders. Can you tell who has a positive body image and who has a negative one? The answers appear below (careful—some may be tricky).

As part of a body-image survey, the teens were instructed to make a picture of themselves. Those who said they didn't like their appearance often drew unflattering portraits with exaggerated features. Girls with a poor body image frequently gave themselves overly large stomachs, hips, and thighs, while dissatisfied boys felt they were either too thin or too fat overall. On the other hand, boys and girls who were content with their body types created drawings that were more accurate in proportion and showed their subjects as being happier.

Many participants indicated that they liked their bodies "sometimes," admitting that while they had many good features, there were some things they'd like to change. As your body grows and develops, this attitude is perfectly natural. (Here's a hint to the quiz: there may be a few "sometimes" teens among these portraits.)

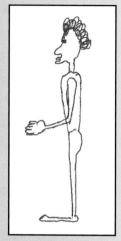

Figure A

Figure E

Figure B

Figure C

Figure D

Figure F

Figure G

Figure H

The Road to Eating Disorders

Three

One afternoon during basketball practice, Kendra's coach yelled at the team for its sluggish play. "It's all that junk food slowin' you down," he said, referring to the corn chips some of the girls had been munching on before turnout. Although Kendra could see her coach wasn't really angry, she felt bad. Jogging down the court, Kendra vowed never to eat before practice again. Better yet, she would go on a strict diet to show her coach that she was a serious player. For two days, Kendra ate only salad and low-salt crackers. She drank herbal tea and water. By the third day of her diet, she was weak, dizzy, irritable, and had diarrhea.

She had such a bad headache that her mom had to pick her up during school. "I almost passed out," Kendra recalls. "It really scared me. And I missed a really important away game."

Fortunately, Kendra stopped her diet before things got worse. Skipping meals, fasting, dieting, overeating, and over exercising are signs of what is called disordered eating. Disordered eating is not the same as an eating disorder, but it can become one if left unchecked. Disordered eating means that a person's attitudes about food, body image, and weight are causing him or her to set up strict exercise and eating habits. This kind of behavior may put someone's health at risk. In a small number of cases, disordered eating may lead to a full-blown eating disorder. Experts estimate that about 80 percent of Americans engage in some kind of disordered eating, meaning only one in five of us have a healthy relationship with food. Most of those who have an eating disorder say their illness was born from disordered eating—usually a diet—that got out of control.

Emotional Hunger

"I started eating a lot more three years ago, about the time my parents got divorced," says Alec, a sixth grader. "My mom and dad were fighting all the time. I guess it just made me feel better to eat when I got nervous or upset. Besides, when you're eating, you don't have to think about anything except for how good the food tastes."

Want to *Gain* Weight? Go on a Diet

Today, The American Dietetic Association (ADA) estimates that more than 50 percent of adults and 25 percent of kids are above their target weight range—statistics that have doubled in just the last twelve years. Some of the reasons for this include decreased activity levels, poor nutritional choices, and pressure from advertisers, who spend $8 billion a year selling prepackaged foods, snacks, and sugary drinks.

Nutritionists say one of the biggest factors in America's expanding waistline may be the very thing we rely on to drop pounds: diets. A diet involves restricting or avoiding particular foods for a certain length of time, often depriving the body of important nutrients. To survive on fewer calories, the body slows metabolism—the process by which food is converted into energy. Dehydration (the loss of water and vital fluids) occurs. Fat as well as muscle is burned as fuel.

Eventually, most people realize the rigid rules of a diet are simply too unrealistic to follow for long. They end the diet and return to previous eating patterns. However, the body, which has now learned to survive in starvation mode, does not need more calories. It begins to pack on the pounds. Within weeks, dieters are often shocked to find that they are five or ten pounds above their original pre-diet weight.

Scientists have also found that each of us has a set point, a preprogrammed weight range the body tries to maintain. Genetics and brain chemistry help to determine our set point. After dieting, the body will deliberately add extra pounds past the set point to protect itself from future starvation. Research shows that 95 percent of dieters gain back all the weight they have lost within five years of their diet.

Do you ever find yourself eating when you're not even hungry? Or not eating when you are? Often, the decisions we make about food—what to eat, why to eat, and when to eat—are based not on a growling stomach but on our emotions. We may eat when we're sad, happy, lonely, angry, stressed, or bored. Since we aren't always able to control what happens to us in life, we may find relief in the one thing we always have control over: food. Just because you eat when you're a bit emotional doesn't mean you will develop an eating disorder. But when you use food to feel better, you are avoiding dealing with what is really bothering you.

People who develop eating disorders may be looking for ways to fill an emotional need or cope with a difficult situation. They may use food to try to gain control when nothing else works.

"My ED [eating disorder] was my great escape," says Colette, a recovering anorexic and bulimic. "I didn't have to deal with guys asking, or not asking, me out. I just wanted to withdraw from life—to stay in my room, sleep, and be left alone."

Who Is at Risk?

No one knows for sure why eating disorders occur. But researchers have found that genetics, brain chemistry, cultural influences, and family issues are contributing factors. A stressful event or the onset of bodily changes at puberty may also open the door to anorexia, bulimia, or binge eating disorder. There is no way of determining who will get an eating disorder, but studies have found that people with eating disorders share some similar qualities. Among them are:

- low self-esteem and negative body image
- excessive concern with food, weight, and exercise
- a strong drive for perfection
- pressure to succeed or high family expectations
- lack of friends and supportive relationships
- emotional sensitivity
- depression or anxiety
- a family history of eating disorders, dieting, obesity, or depression

Eating disorders primarily affect Caucasian girls and women, but statistics show that they are steadily increasing among boys and men. Today, one out of every ten people with an eating disorder is male. People who participate in activities or professions in which weight is key to success are more likely to develop an eating disorder. This includes dancers, models, musicians, actors, and athletes such as gymnasts, jockeys, wrestlers, bodybuilders, swimmers, and figure skaters.

While some groups may be more at risk than others, it is important to remember that eating disorders cross all class, cultural, and religious boundaries. An eating disorder can strike anyone, of any age, at any time.

Four

Anorexia: A Downward Spiral

I n the spring of seventh grade, twelve-year-old Amanda was hit by a series of devastating setbacks. First, a fire burned her home to the ground. Then, due to a family member's allergies, she had to give away her beloved dog. But the worst blow of all came the day Amanda learned her mother had cancer. In the midst of so much turmoil, Amanda wanted to do something good for herself. She resolved to eat better and get into shape. The 5-foot (152-cm), 105-pound (48-kg) honor student didn't need to lose weight. But she saw a cute swimsuit in a magazine, which reminded her that summer was just a month away. She figured dropping a few pounds couldn't hurt.

Triggering a Deadly Disease

Many factors can stir up the negative stress that can lead to anorexia. Among them are trying to be a perfect student, not having enough time to yourself, feeling pressure to be everyone's best friend, early body development, divorce, moving, starting a new school, and the illness/death of a parent or family member.

The athlete and A student tackled her diet the way she handled everything else in her life: with firm commitment. At first, Amanda stopped consuming sweets, chips, and soft drinks. She restricted herself to low-fat foods. As she began to lose weight, Amanda felt a sense of accomplishment. Her friends said she looked great, which only encouraged her to continue dieting. Soon Amanda was cutting back on low-fat foods until she was barely eating anything at all.

Amanda's parents were the first to notice her 10-pound (5-kg) weight loss. And they weren't happy about it. "I can't remember a time during that summer when we weren't fighting at the dinner table about my eating," says Amanda. "My dad got pretty angry. Sometimes, my parents would say I couldn't leave the table unless I ate everything on my plate. I'd hide food under the table and say I'd eaten it, just so they would leave me alone. That was the worst part—lying to my parents."

The Face of Anorexia

Anorexia is a Greek word meaning "a loss of desire to eat," and *nervosa* is Latin for "nervous." Together, anorexia nervosa means "a loss of appetite due to a psychological illness." This is a bit confusing because those with anorexia nervosa (anorexia, for short) have not really lost their appetite. As the disease progresses, however, this often happens. People with anorexia starve themselves, causing significant weight loss. The main symptoms of anorexia nervosa include:

- refusal to eat enough to maintain a healthy body weight
- a loss of at least 15 percent of body weight
- intense fear of gaining weight
- distorted body image; insists there's excess body fat where none exists and/or is preoccupied with body image
- amenorrhea—absence of a menstrual cycle for three or more months; a delayed menstrual cycle for girls who have yet to start their period

Although British physician Sir William Gull first coined the term in 1874, anorexia did not gain public notoriety until the latter half of the 1900s. Most people had never heard of anorexia when thirty-two-year-old pop singer Karen Carpenter died of the illness in 1983 (her years of self-starvation led to heart failure). Today, it is a different story. One in every one hundred adolescents will find themselves in a life-and-death struggle with anorexia.

Anorexics restrict their food intake, even though they may feel intense hunger pains and spend much of their day thinking about food. You know that if you eat a handful of potato chips you will not gain 5 pounds (2 kg). But persons who are anorexic do not see it that way. They are afraid of getting fat and afraid of the one thing that will make them fat: food.

Anorexics frequently have a distorted view of their bodies. They may look into the mirror and see a fat person, when they are really nothing but skin and bones. Amanda was different because she knew she was getting too thin.

Anorexics may look into the mirror and see a fat person, when they are really nothing but skin and bones.

"It was crazy. It made no sense," she recalls. "I was even afraid to put on flavored lip gloss because I didn't want to gain weight. It was a downward spiral. I got scared because I couldn't get myself to eat."

Starving to Death

As the summer wore on, Amanda noticed some frightening symptoms. When she ran her fingers through her hair, clumps of hair would come out in her hands. She was always cold, even on the hottest August day. Fine, downy hairs called lanugo grew all over her body. The skin on her palms and her feet turned yellow. Feeling tired, cranky, and unable to concentrate, Amanda withdrew to her room to spend most of the day sleeping.

Amanda didn't realize that the symptoms she was experiencing were from malnutrition. Her severe dieting had caused her to lose a layer of protective fat. It had also lowered her core body temperature, which is why she felt cold all the time. The lanugo was her body's desperate attempt to try to insulate her. Her mood swings, lethargy, and poor concentration were due to biochemical imbalances and low blood sugar. When you don't eat enough, your brain and body are forced to run on adrenaline, a hormone that is released when you are stressed or fearful.

Some of the more serious health consequences of anorexia include: shrinkage of brain tissue, kidney damage or failure, liver damage or failure, stomach and digestive-tract problems, delayed growth and development, infertility, increased susceptibility to infection, brittle bones and osteoporosis (a disease in which bones become very fragile), irregular heartbeat, low blood pressure, stroke, heart attack, and heart failure. Between 10 and 20 percent of those with long-term anorexia die, either from medical complications—such as heart or organ failure—or from suicide. Anorexia has

Family Ties, Especially for Guys

About half of all females with anorexia have a relative with an eating disorder, but the genetic link appears to be even stronger for males. Research shows that boys and men with anorexia have twice as many relatives with eating disorders as female anorexics.

the highest death rate of any mental illness. It is also the leading cause of death in females fifteen to twenty-four years old.

In the fall, a depressed, sickly, and ever-shivering Amanda started back to school. Too weak to participate in physical education or sports, she had to drop out of basketball and soccer. Amanda kept to herself most of the time, no longer wanting to hang out with her friends or get involved in school activities. When confronted by her teacher and the school principal, Amanda finally admitted what she had been doing. She had been too scared to ask for help. Her parents enrolled Amanda in outpatient therapy, but she resisted treatment. She found ways around the weigh-ins and wouldn't follow the nutritional plan from her dietitian. In October, five months after she began her original diet to lose a few pounds, Amanda was rushed to the hospital emergency room by her mom and dad. Her blood pressure had dropped dangerously low, and she was severely dehydrated. Amanda was hospitalized weighing just 72 pounds (33 kg).

Out of the Darkness

For two months, Amanda underwent residential, or live-in, treatment at an eating-disorders clinic. Slowly, with the help of a team of understanding doctors, counselors, and nutritionists, Amanda began her journey toward recovery. She had to relearn how to listen to her body's signals for food and change her views toward food and life.

Someone with an eating disorder must come to terms with the fact that their eating disorder is not a solution to the problem but "the biggest problem of all," explains Dr. Rosemary Calderon, Clinical Care Coordinator of the Eating Disorders Program at Children's Hospital and Regional Medical Center in Seattle, Washington. "The key to recovery is to help people get back in touch with who they were and what they liked about their lives before the illness, while offering real skills to address the concerns that may have precipitated the eating disorder."

In Amanda's case, that meant discovering how to communicate with others, instead of keeping her feelings locked inside. It meant seeing her body in a new light and realizing that perfectionism was an unattainable

"The key to recovery is to help people get back in touch with who they were and what they liked about their lives before the illness."

goal. Amanda was taught techniques to deal with stress, such as deep breathing and relaxation. For many patients, recovery may also involve coming face to face with difficult family issues, rather than masking them with an eating disorder.

Today, Amanda is back home with her family and has returned to school. Her weight is within the normal range for her height. Doctors say she should have no long-term health effects from her anorexia. Recovery isn't easy; some days are still a struggle. Amanda says she will always be sensitive around food. But she has learned to be comfortable with herself, confident in her spirit, and caring of her body. "I'm not so hard on myself anymore," she says. "I don't have to be perfect; I just have to be me. When I look back on that summer, I realize I was self-conscious. I would never give my opinion. Now I say what I think—maybe too much sometimes," laughs Amanda. "It's like I have finally found my real personality. And every day I'm finding my true self more and more."

Battling Bulimia and Binge Eating

I n 1970, Cathy Rigby became the first female American gymnast to win a medal in international competition. For her sparkling performance on the balance beam at the World Gymnastics Championships, Cathy earned a silver medal. But behind the blonde pigtails, pixie body, and winning smile, the seventeen-year-old athlete hid a dark secret: She suffered from bulimia.

Two years earlier, at the Summer Olympics in Mexico City, Cathy earned the highest all-around score ever given to an American woman. But, like any teen, her body was growing and developing. It was getting tougher to maintain the 90-pound (41-kg) weight limit her coach had set for her. Even though Cathy was eating just one meal a day, she was still gaining weight. The changes in her body were slowing her down on the apparatus. Her coach urged her to lose weight. So Cathy began throwing up whatever she ate. "I'd always let others— my father, my coach, the judges—make my decisions for me," she said in an interview. "They determined how

I felt. If I stayed skinny and got a good score, I was good. If I gained weight and I didn't score well, I was bad. But I didn't have the confidence to take responsibility for any of it."

At age nineteen, when Cathy left the spotlight with twelve international medals, eight of them gold, she could not leave her bulimia behind. She was hospitalized twice with complications from the disease and nearly died of heart failure. In the early 1980s, twelve years after the onset of her bulimia, Cathy finally sought professional treatment. Today, she is free of her eating disorder and is a successful mother, actress, and sports commentator.

The Secret World of Bulimia Nervosa

Bulimia nervosa, often shortened to bulimia, is a repeated pattern of bingeing—eating a large amount of food—and then purging—getting rid of the food. First identified by doctors in the late 1970s, *bulimia* is Greek for "oxlike hunger," referring to the gorging aspect of the disease. Like anorexia, bulimia is a mental illness, so it is coupled with the Latin word for "nervous," *nervosa*.

A binge usually involves eating anywhere between 1,000 and 10,000 calories at a time, though behavior can vary widely. While one person may gorge on thousands

Elisa's Diary

In 1989, thirteen year-old Elisa McCall went on a diet to lose weight for gymnastics, unaware that her quest to drop a few pounds would lead to a life and death struggle with bulimia. In the following excerpts from her journal, the 20-year old college student wrote a letter to herself from the point of view of her eating disorder, and another letter in response.

Dear Elisa:

I am your eating disorder. I am your excuse, your outlet for pain ... I numb your feelings and make you warm inside. I protect you from the world, which can be so bitter and heartless... I make you crazy. I make nothing else matter. And, if you don't let go, I will make you die.

From the first time I spoke to you, "You're gonna be a fat girl and you're only 13. Better watch it!" I spoke to you when boys started to notice you. "Suck in your tummy! They're watching you. No one is going to like you if you don't have a perfect body." I've said the most horrible things anyone had ever said to you and you've listened as if I were God. You've taken it all to heart and let it shape and mold who you are today. I control your life.

In order to get rid of me you must stop listening to my terrible voice ... You must learn to love yourself and stop waiting for my acceptance ... for I will never approve. It is possible for you to exist without me.

Signed,
    Your Eating Disorder

Dear Eating Disorder:

You have been my life for the past six years. You are heartless and mean and I am sorry I ever started listening to you. You preyed upon me when I was young and naive. You gave me my own safe world ... But I am no longer that little girl in need of your protection.

I want to experience it all, good and bad without you as my armor, for I'm working on my own protective shield. It is the shield of experience and it grows thicker everyday. So, I'm discarding you because your services are no longer wanted or needed. I don't need you to define my self-worth or direct my life anymore. I will get rid of you one of these days. It's been a long process, but you are fading away slowly.

Elisa

A few months later, Elisa McCall took her own life. She left her journal to her father, and asked him to use her story to save other teens from becoming caught in the deadly grip of eating disorders. In Elisa's memory, her family established The Elisa Project, _www.TheElisaProject.org_.

of calories in a half hour, another may slowly eat a regular-size meal. In all cases, bulimics get rid of what they have eaten. Purging may include vomiting or the use of diuretics, laxatives, and enemas. A bulimic may also purge by fasting or over exercising to burn off the consumed calories. The major symptoms of bulimia nervosa include:

- repeated episodes of secretive bingeing and purging
- feeling out of control during a binge
- purging after a binge to prevent weight gain through self-induced vomiting, laxatives, diet pills, diuretics, excessive exercise, and/or fasting
- extreme concern with body weight and shape

Many of the same emotions and issues that trigger anorexia are also found in bulimia: the need for control, a fear of getting fat, a distorted body image, the quest for perfection, depression, and/or anxiety. Researchers have found that as many as two-thirds of anorexics will become bulimic. Anorexics may turn to bulimia when starvation doesn't seem to be achieving the results they want. Also, the natural drive to eat may be so strong that they mistakenly view bingeing and purging as a way to satisfy their hunger without gaining weight.

What bulimics often do not realize is that the laxatives, diuretics, and enemas they use to purge do not work. Laxatives clear out the large intestine, not the small intestine, where most of the nutrients from food are absorbed. The dehydration that follows the use of diuretics and enemas may make bulimics mistakenly feel they have dropped weight when, in fact, only water has been lost. And the body quickly replenishes any water that has been flushed out of the system.

Julia, now a college sophomore, began her fight with anorexia in sixth grade. In four years, she starved off 55 pounds (25 kg), dropping dangerously below her normal weight range. In high school, she turned to bulimia. "Why did I binge? Because I was hungry and I couldn't stand it anymore," Julia admits. As part of her purging ritual, Julia exercised to the extreme, going to the gym for

Addicted to Exercise

Some people exercise compulsively, either as part of their eating disorder or because they are addicted to working out (which can sometimes lead to an eating disorder). Some of the warning signs of exercise addiction include extended workout sessions that last for an hour or more, forcing yourself to do an exercise that you don't enjoy, and not being able to skip a daily workout even when you're sick, injured, or tired. If you simply have to exercise, no matter what, you may have a problem with exercise addiction.

two hours every day. She also joined the track, basketball, swimming, and water-polo teams.

The majority of bulimics are female, but up to 15 percent of those with the disease are male. Bulimia is often harder to identify than anorexia because a person with the disease is usually at or just above their normal weight. Also, since they may eat normally in public, no one may be aware of their dangerous cycle of bingeing and purging.

Some of bulimia's physical symptoms include fatigue, headaches, iron deficiency (anemia), swollen cheeks, and irregular menstrual cycles. Throwing up repeatedly can cause bleeding in the throat and stomach. The acids in vomit can wear away teeth and damage the esophagus, the tube that connects the back of the mouth to the stomach. The repeated abuse of laxatives may lead to intestinal problems, including no longer being able to control the bowels. Purging also robs the body of vital minerals called electrolytes. Electrolytes, such as potassium and sodium, help transmit nerve impulses throughout the body. Electrolyte imbalances may cause brain seizures and heart failure.

Eventually, Julia ended up in an intensive-care unit. Her potassium level was so low that doctors feared she could have a heart attack at any minute. "I was told a million times that if I threw up one more time, I'd die, and I did it anyway," recalls Julia. "I didn't think I'd really die—until it almost happened."

Behind Binge Eating

Those with binge eating disorder (BED) may eat up to 10,000 calories, either gorging a large amount of food at once or continuously eating over a period of time. Binge eaters may want to purge, like a bulimic, but cannot or will not make themselves throw up. Instead, they may fast or diet to try to lose weight.

Binge eating disorder is a mental illness fueled by some of the same emotions and issues that cause other eating disorders, such as anxiety, loneliness, depression, and poor body image. Experts say it may also be triggered by diets. Restricting certain foods can create overwhelming cravings, which lead to out-of-control eating, which then leads to fasting and more dieting, thereby keeping the abusive cycle in motion.

Binge eating disorder is fueled by the same emotions and issues that cause other eating disorders, such as anxiety, loneliness, depression, and poor body image.

Binge eaters usually choose sweets or other high-fat, high-calorie foods. Many of their symptoms are similar to those found in people who are obese (defined as being 30 percent or more above their ideal weight range). Some of the health risks of binge eating are high cholesterol, diabetes, high blood pressure, stroke, and heart disease.

Some of the symptoms of binge eating disorder are:

- a frequent pattern of eating an amount of food much larger than a normal person would eat at one sitting or eating continuously over a period of time
- eating food without tasting it or without regard to hunger
- bingeing in secret
- feeling out of control during bingeing, then feeling ashamed or guilty when it is over
- self-loathing and negative body image
- depression, guilt, or loneliness
- repeated failures at dieting

People with BED may appear to be within their normal weight range, extremely overweight, or anywhere in between. Athletes are particularly at risk for binge eating. A study by the National Collegiate Athletic Association (NCAA) found that 13 percent of college-age male athletes and 10 percent of female athletes binge-eat at least once a week. Because they may fast, diet, or work off calories through exercise, there may not be noticeable weight gain.

Unlike anorexia and bulimia, which affect primarily females, as many as 40 percent of binge eaters are male.

"I can't remember a time in my life when I didn't have a problem with overeating," says Tom. "I was a big kid for my age, taller and wider than everybody else. By the time I started junior high, I weighed over 300 pounds (136 kg). Kids teased me and I was shy anyway, so my body image went right into the toilet. I was a grazer; I never stopped eating all day long. Breakfast would be toast, eggs, bacon, cereal—you name it, I ate it." Tom turned to bulimia to try to control his weight, which only made things worse. He went back and forth from bulimic behavior (purging through vomiting and over exercising) to binge eating. Tom's weight shifted up and down, sometimes fluctuating 10 pounds (5 kg) or more in a matter of days. His electrolytes were constantly out of balance, and his heart rate dipped to a low level. After years of abusing his body, Tom sought help from Overeaters Anonymous, a self-help support program for people struggling with food issues. Today, he no longer struggles with eating disorders. He now has a positive body image and a healthy relationship with food.

Reaching Out

Maggie knew something was wrong. Her best friend, Beth, had not been herself lately. She seemed to be disappearing under her thick, wool sweaters like a turtle into its shell. Beth's bright eyes were now sad as if, somehow, the life were draining out of them. Beth didn't play softball anymore. She rarely went to dance class and had stopped going over to Maggie's house after school to make nachos and watch television. When Maggie asked her friend what was wrong, Beth would say "nothing."

"I shut everyone out," says thirteen-year-old Beth, when she looks back on her life before she found treatment for her anorexia. "I ruined everything—grades, sports, friendships. When you have an eating disorder, your life *is* the disorder. But eventually, you face it. You have to. Either you face it or you die."

Shame, guilt, and the mental confusion that accompany malnutrition are some of the main reasons why those with eating disorders do not seek help. Fear can be one of the biggest obstacles. Fear of getting fat, fear of being judged, or fear of not knowing what the treatment will entail can prevent a person from reaching out. Also, many people with eating disorders do not recognize that there is a problem and so do not feel there is any reason to get treatment. This is called denial. Denial is more than refusing to admit something is true. It is the inability to actually see the truth. "You

"You're fat, and no one can convince you otherwise, because that is what you know, not just believe, to be true."

look in the mirror," explains Kristen, age twelve, "and you're fat. It's there; that's what's in the mirror, even though you've lost 30 pounds (14 kg). You're fat, and no one can convince you otherwise, because that is what you *know*, not just believe, to be true."

Is Something Eating You?

Ask yourself these questions to see if you may be at risk for developing an eating disorder:

- *Do you have to know the calorie count or fat content of everything you eat?*
- *Are you terrified of being overweight or having fat on your body?*
- *When you're exercising, do you think about how many calories you are burning instead of enjoying the experience?*
- *Are friends and family constantly telling you that you're too thin?*
- *Are you continually dieting?*
- *Do you have to weigh yourself every day?*

Answering "yes" to any of the above questions doesn't necessarily mean you will get an eating disorder. But it would be wise to reconsider your attitudes toward food and your body. If at any time you feel your eating habits are out of control, talk to your parents, family doctor, or a counselor immediately.

Telling Secrets

Family and friends are often the first to spot the signs of an eating disorder, such as rapid weight loss, changes in personality, or food quickly disappearing off cabinet shelves. Initially, they may react in various ways, perhaps hoping the person will "grow out of it" or thinking that if they can just get the person to eat, everything will be all right. But a person with an eating disorder has a disease. He or she cannot snap out of it any more than you can cure yourself of a broken leg. Only qualified professionals can treat eating disorders. Experts say recovery depends on early diagnosis and treatment.

Eating Disorders: Warning Signs and Symptoms

Disorder (top) / Clues to Watch For (bottom)	
Anorexia nervosa	Bulimia nervosa
Dramatic weight loss, feeling cold even in warm weather, hair loss, eating or playing with tiny portions of food on their plate, avoiding having to eat with others, unusual eating habits or rituals, lack of interest in previous activities, personality changes, over exercising, hyperactivity, or fatigue	Long time spent in the bathroom after meals, bruised knuckles from self-induced vomiting, damaged teeth, swollen cheeks or sore throat, sudden disappearance of large amounts of food, mood swings, laxative or diuretic wrappers in the trash, over exercising

"If you don't intervene early on and the child is young at the age of onset, then it is probably more damaging over the long course, just because it becomes so enmeshed with their developing personalities," says Dr. Rosemary Calderon. "We are seeing ED's (eating disorders) in younger and younger children, so, hopefully, people are keying in to diagnosing it early and referring the child for treatment rather than waiting to see if the child 'grows out of it.'"

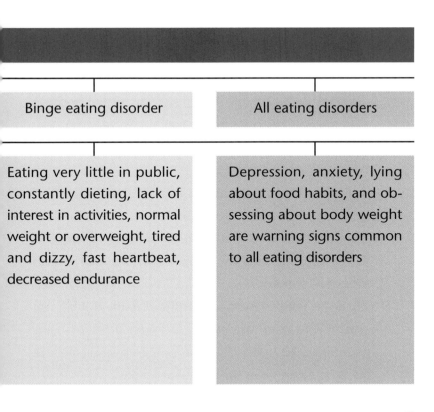

Binge eating disorder	All eating disorders
Eating very little in public, constantly dieting, lack of interest in activities, normal weight or overweight, tired and dizzy, fast heartbeat, decreased endurance	Depression, anxiety, lying about food habits, and obsessing about body weight are warning signs common to all eating disorders

What should you do if you suspect that a friend has an eating disorder? The most important thing is not to wait until your friend's life is in danger. Time is critical. Every day the illness goes unchecked is one more day that health damage is occurring. Here are some tips that may help you talk to him or her now:

- Find a quiet place to discuss things with your friend.
- Be kind, calm, and gentle. Don't get mad or place blame.
- In a caring way, point out a few specific instances you've seen that have caused you to worry. Use "I" statements, rather than the more accusatory "you" statements. You might say, "I am concerned because you haven't been eating at lunch," instead of "You look sick" or "You need help," which may make your friend defensive or angry.
- Tell your friend you think this is a problem that needs professional attention. Encourage him or her to tell a school counselor, parent, or doctor. Offer to go along for support when your friend does tell someone.
- Listen to your friend's feelings and fears. But do not promise to keep the eating disorder a secret. Your friend may be in denial, afraid to tell, or falsely believe he or she can solve the problem alone.

- If your friend refuses to seek help, you need to tell his or her parents immediately.

Hope and Help

Getting help for an eating disorder is not something to be scared of. The most successful treatment involves a caring, compassionate team of professionals who can work together to help heal the mind and body.

Because eating disorders are complicated illnesses, recovery can take from a few months to many years. Most eating disorders can be treated on an outpatient basis, meaning regular visits to doctors, therapists, and nutritionists. Sometimes, inpatient therapy, or a short hospital stay, is needed. Occasionally, the illness has progressed to the point where admission to a residential, or "live-in," treatment program at a center specializing in eating disorders is necessary. A patient may need to stay in the treatment center for one to six months or, in some cases, longer.

Embarrassed to Death

Studies show males are far less likely to seek help for eating disorders than females. They fear being judged for what is often regarded as a "girls-only" disease. Not only is this dangerous thinking, but it is also inaccurate. Today, one out of every six new patients diagnosed with anorexia is male.

Each year, about nine thousand people are hospitalized for treatment of eating disorders. During recovery, physicians treat the physical aspects of the disease, such as vitamin deficiencies, dental problems, and other health complications. They work to restore the patient to a normal weight. Drugs to help depression or anxiety may also be prescribed. Nutritionists design individualized eating plans and steer a patient toward the realization that there are no "good" or "bad" foods.

Psychotherapy is a way for people to sort through their problems by discussing their feelings with a qualified professional. A psychotherapist, or therapist, helps a patient explore personal and family issues, and suggests solutions. A therapist can also pinpoint unhealthy thoughts, attitudes, and behaviors that contribute to an eating disorder. Through therapy, patients learn new ways of thinking and strategies for coping with the disorder.

"Therapy is always about helping you with your goals," stresses Carolyn Costin, founder and clinical director of the Monte Nido Residential Treatment Center in Malibu, California. Costin, who went through therapy and recovered from anorexia twenty years ago, now works as a therapist and educator. She advises kids, "You should like your therapist and actually feel like you want to go to therapy. This does not mean it always has to be fun or feel good, but it does mean that the person is someone you trust. Think of your therapist as a person you hire to help you. In the beginning, you may not feel this is true, especially if you are afraid to give up some of your behaviors. In the long run, however, no one can make you stop doing anything or give up anything. Hopefully, they can help you to see what serves you and what does not serve you and how to know the difference."

"If it weren't for my therapist, I can tell you flat out I wouldn't be here today," says Lauren, who went through more than a year of residential therapy in her struggle with anorexia and bulimia. "I had to face that I was lovable, that I could love myself and someone else could love me, too. I am still scared, but now I have knowledge, support, and love. Hope is still present."

Family therapy, which includes the entire family of someone with an eating disorder, can also aid in recovery. With guidance from a therapist, families learn how to handle stress, express their feelings, and relate to one another in healthier, more productive ways.

Even with a good treatment program, many patients will relapse, or fall back into old self-destructive patterns, at least once during their recovery. Within two years of beginning treatment, however, 80 to 90 percent of those with eating disorders make significant progress. Over time, more than half of all patients will fully recover.

Seven

Changing the View

Remember the definition of body image? It's how you mentally picture your body and how you feel in your skin. When you look in the mirror are you confident or critical? Self-assured or self-conscious? Because body image is perception, not reality, you have the ability to alter your point of view by changing your thought cycle.

Here's how it works: Every thought that crosses your mind triggers a particular feeling. Every feeling you have calls you to some kind of action, which fuels another thought, which creates another feeling, which urges you to action once again. The negative cycle might start with something like, "My thighs are too fat. I can't wear shorts." Naturally, thoughts like this are likely to make you feel frustrated and sad. Perhaps it may cause you to pass up something you really want to do, like playing on the volleyball team because you don't think you will look good in the uniform. This action is likely to spark another negative thought, which creates more disapproving feelings and more inaction. Before you know it, your self-esteem—your belief in your worth as a person—begins to plummet. If left to continue, the negative thought cycle might cause you to withdraw from friends, stop participating in life, and become depressed.

So how do you break a negative cycle? When defeating thoughts occur, you can counter them with positive messages. The response to your concern about your thighs might be, "My thighs are strong and muscular, which is why I am good at volleyball." Changing your point of view can help you feel hopeful and confident. Since feelings are what fuel actions, a positive thought is likely to give birth to a positive action. Feeling powerful, encouraged, and happy, you are less apt to focus on how you look in shorts and can focus instead on playing volleyball because you enjoy it.

Altering your thoughts doesn't mean pretending everything is wonderful when it isn't. But when it comes

The Thought Cycle

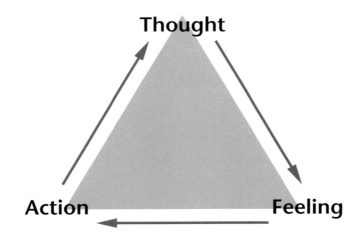

Negative Cycle

Thought: *My thighs are too fat. I can't wear shorts.*
Feelings: Frustration, anger, sadness
Action: Don't wear shorts: don't play volleyball

Positive Cycle

Thought: *My thighs are strong and muscular. I am a good volleyball player.*
Feelings: Hopeful, confident, powerful, happy
Action: Wear shorts: play volleyball

to your body image, you can put a stop to the "put down" cycle by giving yourself positive, believable messages to act on. This can put you on the path toward accomplishing your goals and dreams, while learning to

You can put a stop to the "put down" cycle by giving yourself positive, believable messages to act on.

love yourself for who you are. Here are some additional steps you can take to ensure that your body image stays on the "plus" side:

- Surround yourself with people who support, respect, and love you. Choose your friends and dates carefully. Stay away from anyone who puts you down, and never remain in a verbally or physically abusive relationship.

- Don't engage in negative body talk. If your friends start criticizing their bodies, tell them it bothers you. Take the word "fat" out of your own vocabulary.

- Communicate. It's all right to express yourself to friends and family when you are sad, hurt, or angry. Use "I" messages, rather than "you" messages, which can put others on the defensive. You might say, "I feel hurt when you make fun of my clothes because I like the way I dress." Tell others what you expect from them, such as, "I need for you to accept me just the way I am."

- Stress can play a big role in how you view yourself. Positive stress can help you take action, solve problems, and accomplish goals. It can motivate you, like the butterflies you get before a speech or recital. Negative stress—such as a divorce in the family, breaking up with a girlfriend or boyfriend, or problems at school—can fuel the negative thought cycle. When you feel stressed out, look for ways to relax. Deep breathing, listening to quiet music, a short workout, a warm bath, or yoga are some of the ways you can relieve the pressure.

- Stop comparing yourself to the airbrushed, computer-enhanced media images that aren't real. In fact, don't compare yourself to anyone. Celebrate that you are one of a kind, with unique talents and abilities. And toss out the scale!

Like a painting or sculpture, your body image is your own individual work of art. In defining who you are, you can choose to highlight your flaws or focus on the fabulous. You have the power of creation because you have the power of choice.

Body-Image Boosters

The next time you are tempted to get down on yourself, try one of these ideas to fire up your body image:

- *Start a journal. Keep track of your good qualities, achievements, and all the things you have to be thankful for. Write down your dreams and goals.*
- *The next time someone compliments you, don't say, "Oh, no, I'm not that good." Accept it with a smile and say, "Thanks!"*
- *Try an activity you've never done before but always wanted to do, like playing tennis, drawing, or writing poetry. Even if you make lots of mistakes, congratulate yourself for having the courage to try something new.*
- *Who is your hero? How has he or she inspired you? Look honestly at the role appearance has played in his or her achievements.*
- *Find and appreciate the beauty that surrounds you every day. Enjoy viewing a sky filled with fluffy clouds, reading a kind note from a friend, or snuggling with your pet.*

Eating Smart for Life

Food and body image go hand in hand. Your relationship with food plays a key role in your body image. And your body image has an enormous impact on what you decide to eat. By developing healthy attitudes toward food, you can steer clear of disordered eating like dieting and fasting. You can also avoid getting entangled in the web of an eating disorder.

Have you ever skipped breakfast? How do you feel a couple of hours later? You probably feel tired and find it hard to think clearly, especially with all the grumbling going on in your stomach. From your skeleton to your skin, every cell in your body depends on the nutrients in food to survive, grow, and fight disease. Each day, you need an ample supply of carbohydrates, proteins, fats, vitamins, minerals, and water to stay active and healthy.

This is why it is important to eat a wide variety of foods from each of the groups in the U.S. Department of Agriculture's Food Guide Pyramid. At the bottom of the pyramid are those foods that should make up most of your daily diet: breads, cereals, rice, and pasta. Foods at the top of the pyramid—oils, fats, and sweets—should be eaten sparingly. Most kids need to eat the number of servings from the low to the middle range of each category, such as six to nine servings from the breads and cereals group.

Good nutrition doesn't have to be difficult if you remember a few basic things. First, there are no "good" or "bad" foods. Some foods have higher amounts of fat or sugar, while others may be higher in protein or fiber. If you have some fat, protein, carbohydrates, and two to

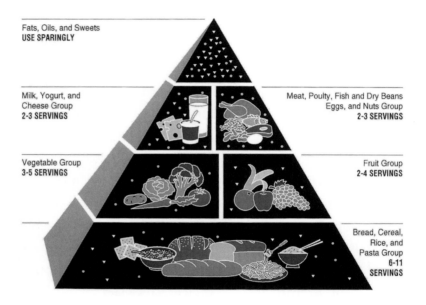

Fats, Oils, and Sweets
USE SPARINGLY

Milk, Yogurt, and
Cheese Group
2-3 SERVINGS

Meat, Poulty, Fish and Dry Beans
Eggs, and Nuts Group
2-3 SERVINGS

Vegetable Group
3-5 SERVINGS

Fruit Group
2-4 SERVINGS

Bread, Cereal,
Rice, and
Pasta Group
6-11
SERVINGS

three kinds of fruits and vegetables a day, then you will be giving your mind and body the fuel they need. Eating a variety of foods not only supplies your body with a wide range of nutrients from different sources, but it also entices your taste buds and makes eating fun. Also, don't feed emotional hunger. Instead of munching when you're bored, sad, or stressed, find another activity to brighten your mood, such as reading, listening to music, or playing sports. Eat when you're hungry, and stop when you're full. Keep in mind that it can take up to twenty minutes after you eat for your stomach to tell your brain you've had enough. Finally, always be

Get Movin' and Shakin'

Regular exercise helps you stay strong, keeps your weight normal, lifts your mood, and reduces the risk of diabetes and heart disease. The American College of Sports Medicine's Physical Activity Pyramid recommends at least 20 minutes of aerobic exercise three to five times a week (aerobics are exercises that get and keep your heart rate up for an extended length of time). A few times a week, do some strength-building exercises like push-ups, sit-ups, or karate.

"Finding fun and enjoyable physical activities will encourage them to become lifelong habits," advises Sheah Rarbach, registered dietician and spokesman for the American Dietetic Association. "Being active needs to be joyful, not drudgeful." So pick an activity you like—and move!

sure to drink lots of water with and between meals to keep hydrated and to help with digestion.

A True Reflection

Name three things about your best friend that you like. Chances are that none of the characteristics you just mentioned has anything to do with his or her appearance. So why are we so quick to believe the cultural myth that our own worth lies not in who we are but how we look? Intelligence, compassion, loyalty, honesty, kindness, artistry, and love are just a few of the qualities you have to offer the world that go far beyond your physical features.

"I love to knit sweaters for my family, I always have time to listen to my friends, and someday I want to run my own flower shop," says thirteen-year-old Victoria, a recovering anorexic. "And you know what it took me forever to realize? Not one of those things is determined by a number on the bathroom scale."

Can you accept yourself just the way you are—not when you are 10 pounds (5 kg) thinner or when your nose is straighter? This isn't easy to do in a culture where everything from Barbie dolls to beauty pageants continually tells us that physical perfection matters. If you can look past the fun-house mirrors of media messages, peer pressure, and unrealistic worldly expectations, you will discover that appearance has little to do with your chances for happiness and success in life. Once you realize your true worth lies on the inside, you can begin to accept, honor, and love what is on the outside. You will, at last, be able to see a clear, honest reflection of who you are and all the amazing things you are capable of achieving.

Glossary

adolescence: the preteen and teen years when a person is moving from childhood into adulthood

amenorrhea: the absence of menstrual periods for three months in a row or the delay of the start of a menstrual cycle; often caused by malnutrition resulting from an eating disorder

anorexia nervosa: an eating disorder characterized by self-starvation and the refusal to maintain normal body weight

binge: the consumption of a large amount of food that is more than a normal person would eat in a sitting

binge eating disorder (BED): an eating disorder characterized by repeated episodes of secretive bingeing, or continuous eating over a period of time, without purging body image: a mental picture of how you perceive your body, whether by thinking about it or when looking in the mirror

bulimia nervosa: an eating disorder characterized by repeated cycles of secretive bingeing and purging

dieting: avoiding or restricting certain types of food

disordered eating: fasting, skipping meals, or dieting caused by unhealthy attitudes about food and weight; disordered eating may lead to the more serious condition known as an eating disorder

diuretic: a drug that increases urine discharge; often used by bulimics to purge, in the mistaken belief that it will cause weight loss

eating disorder: a mental illness, such as anorexia, bulimia, or binge eating, where behavior relating to food and/or exercise is out of control

electrolyte imbalance: a life-threatening condition where a person does not have enough minerals to maintain a healthy fluid balance; low potassium levels may lead to heart problems, and low sodium levels produce lethargy and, eventually, seizures electrolytes: chemical conductors in the brain that rely on water and other minerals, such as sodium and potassium, to communicate nerve messages to systems throughout the body

hormones: natural chemicals in the body that regulate human growth and development

lanugo: fine, downy hair that grows all over the body in an effort to protect the body from the effects of starvation; often a symptom of anorexia

laxative: a food or drug that causes looseness of the bowels; often mistakenly used by bulimics to purge

lethargic: the state of lacking energy or interest

metabolism: the process within the body whereby food is broken down and converted into fuel for energy

psychotherapy: in the case of eating disorders, therapy or counseling that seeks to address the mental aspects of the disease through the discussion of emotions, feelings, and issues with a qualified doctor; treatments for eating disorders may include individual, group, and/or family therapy puberty: the stage of physical development where a person becomes sexually mature, usually between the ages of nine and eighteen

purge: to empty the stomach or bowels through self-induced vomiting, drugs, laxatives, or enemas; in the case of eating disorders, purging also includes behaviors such as fasting and over exercising to get rid of unwanted calories

relapse: to fall back, or regress, to the previous symptoms of a destructive behavior, such as an eating disorder

self-esteem: your belief in your overall worth and value as a person

set point: a preprogrammed weight range within each person that is determined by individual genetics, brain chemistry, and other bodily factors

Further Resources

Books

Burby, Liza. *Bulimia Nervosa: The Secret Cycle of Bingeing and Purging.* New York: Rosen Publishing Group, 1998.

Davis, Brangien. *What's Real, What's Ideal: Overcoming a Negative Body Image.* New York: The Rosen Publishing Group, 1998.

Kirkpatrick, Jim and Paul Caldwell. *Eating Disorders: Everything You Need to Know.* Buffalo: Firefly Books, 2001.

Smith, Erica. *Anorexia Nervosa: When Food Is the Enemy.* New York: The Rosen Publishing Group, 1998.

Sneddon, Pamela Shires. *Body Image: A Reality Check.* Berkeley Heights: Enslow Publishers, 1999.

Strada, Jennifer. *Eating Disorders.* San Diego: Lucent Books, 2001.

Videos

NOVA: Dying to Be Thin. PBS Home Video, 2000.

Perfect Illusions: Eating Disorders and the Family. PBS Home Video, 2002.

Self Image: The Fantasy, The Reality. New York, NY: CastleWorks Productions, 1997.

Online Sites and Organizations

American Dietetic Association (ADA)
216 W. Jackson Blvd.
Chicago, IL 60606
(312) 899-0040
(800) 877-1600
www.eatright.org
At the ADA web site, you can explore the ins and outs of nutrition, from reading food labels to improving your eating habits; learn more about a career in the nutrition field; or find a registered dietitian in your area.

KidsHealth

Nemours Children's Clinic

1600 Rockland Rd.

Wilmington, DE 19803

(302) 657-4000

www.kidshealth.org

KidsHealth is a nonprofit organization that provides health information about and for children from birth through adolescence. Check out this web site to find recipes designed especially for kids, learn more about eating disorders and body image, and take an interactive trip through the human body.

National Association of Anorexia Nervosa and Associated Disorders (ANAD)

P. O. Box 7

Highland Park, IL 60035

(847) 831-3438

www.anad.org

Find out who is most at risk for getting an eating disorder, learn to spot the danger signs, and get tips on what to do if someone you know has a problem with food.

National Eating Disorders Association (NEDA)
603 Stewart St., Suite 803
Seattle, WA 98101
(800) 931-2237
www.nationaleatingdisorders.org
The NEDA web site is an excellent resource for in-depth information on anorexia, bulimia, and binge eating disorder. Discover ways to improve your body image and to prevent eating disorders. NEDA also offers referrals to treatment centers in your area.

Overeaters Anonymous
P. O. Box 44020
Rio Rancho, NM 87174
(505) 891-2664
www.overeatersanonymous.org
Overeaters Anonymous is a network of support groups for those who struggle with binge and compulsive eating. The web site provides questions to help you determine if you have a problem with food and offers resources for finding a recovery program near you.

Index

About the Author

Trudi Strain Trueit is an award-winning health and medical broadcast journalist. As a news reporter for KREM-TV (CBS) in Spokane, Washington, her weekly on-air segment, *Your Health,* earned recognition from the Society of Professional Journalists. *Your Health* first introduced Ms. Trueit to the destructive world of eating disorders. Her desire to write more about body-image issues was fueled by a loved one's battle with anorexia and bulimia.

Also a television weather forecaster, Ms. Trueit has written numerous books for Scholastic about nature and wildlife. Among her many titles are *Storm Chasers, Clouds, The Water Cycle, Volcanoes, Earthquakes, Fossils, Snakes, Lizards, Turtles,* and *Octopuses, Squids, and Cuttlefish.* Ms. Trueit has a degree in broadcast journalism. She makes her home in Everett, Washington, with her husband, Bill.

The author thanks the following people, who kindly shared their knowledge and insights about key subjects:

My deepest appreciation to Dr. Rosemary Calderon, Associate Professor at the University of Washington and Clinical Care Coordinator of the Eating Disorders Program at Children's Hospital and Regional Medical Center in Seattle, Washington, for her guidance and expertise.

Special thanks to Karen Dawson, health teacher at Valley View Middle School in Snohomish, Washington; Nancy Boone, health teacher at Cascade High School in Everett, Washington, and their students.